D0396644

HERBS +
FLOWERS

PLANT · GROW · EAT ——————

PIP McCORMAC

Illustrations by Louise O'Reilly

quadrille

THE HERBS

THE FLOWERS

INTRODUCTION

———————

There's a real joy in growing your own herbs and flowers, in using the fat of your land to add flavour to your cooking. Having spent an entire childhood avoiding anything to do with my parent's garden, I've discovered the pride involved in snipping off a sprig and popping it straight into your pot.

And the best thing? It's really pretty easy. This book intends to show you how simple it is, featuring 32 of the most popular herbs and edible flowers, this is all you need to get growing.

A FEW NOTES BEFORE YOU GET OUT YOUR TROWEL

SOIL: For herb and window boxes, the multi-use potting soil you buy in massive bags at DIY warehouses and garden centres will work just fine. Fill your boxes almost to the top, plant your seeds or cuttings and give them a really good drenching with water. Once a week, in summer months, it's worth giving them a capful or two of plant feed, available from the same places as the soil.

CONTAINERS: The larger your containers, the better, though herbs can survive for shorter times in tiny pots of around 5cm (2in) in diameter if you don't have much room. The ideal container gives each plant at least 10cm (4in) of space on all sides, to allow for roots and over-ground growth. Put a layer of stones into the bottom before adding the soil, or make sure there are a couple of little holes in the bottom to allow for draining. Seeds and cuttings can be planted in containers outside unless otherwise stated.

PLANTING SEEDS: Unless the specific guidelines tell you otherwise, all you need to do is sprinkle a row of seeds over the top of the container, covering with a light dusting of soil and giving them a good water. As they start to shoot, separate any that are too close together, leaving a gap of at least 2.5cm (1in) between each plantlet. Then, after a couple of weeks, discard those that look a bit weedy and meek to leave room for the ones that are flourishing, this time with at least 5cm (2in) of space between each.

CUTTINGS: Flowers like lavender and honeysuckle grow best from cuttings rather than seeds. Snip a healthy, non-flowering shoot from an existing plant – you want it to be around 5–10cm (2–4in) long. Keep only one or two pairs of leaves at the tip, dip the bottom in root power and poke the cutting into your container, leaving space around it. Water well and watch it grow. Once it's about 15cm (6in) high, you should pinch off the top two leaves to encourage it to grow outwards – repeat this every 10 days or so.

PLANTS: The fastest way to success, of course, is to buy plants from the garden centre and replant them. Squeeze them out of the pots they come in and gingerly break up the clump of earth that clings to their roots, taking care not to damage the roots. Place them into your container and pat some soil in around them. Water them well and you've got a ready-made garden that you can cook from straight away.

"How lovely is the silence of growing things."

———————————

the
HERBS

CHIVE

—

{Allium schoenoprasum}

CHIVE

TASTES: Strongly like onion.

WHEN TO PLANT:
Early spring to midsummer.

WHEN TO PICK: After a couple of months it will have grown enough for you to be able to slice off most of the chive, leaving just 2cm (¾in) to grow back. Chopping off the edible flower head will encourage more to grow.

HOW TO PLANT: Start growing the chives inside, sprinkling the seeds in a row and then barely covering with soil. Water them well and move them outside once they're 5–6cm (2–2½in) tall – you can carefully dig them up and transplant them to another container if you like, spacing them about 15cm (6in) apart. Although they might disappear in the winter, they are still alive – you can leave them outside and they will grow back again in the spring.

PLANT IT WITH: Chives tend to grow pretty tall, so plant them with squat, equally reedy herbs like dill and thyme.

WORKS PARTICULARLY WELL WITH: Beetroot, chicken, haddock, goat's cheese, parsnip, potatoes, sour cream.

SUBSTITUTE IT WITH: Basil, oregano, winter savory.

CAN BE EATEN: Raw, steamed or cooked in sauces.

DILL

—

{Anethum graveolens}

DILL

TASTES: Soft and sweet,
and similar to caraway.

WHEN TO PLANT:
From April until the end of July.

WHEN TO PICK: Snip off the whole stalk
from mid-June until late September.

HOW TO PLANT: Fill a small or medium-
sized container with soil and create a
groove down the middle with the end
of a pencil or your finger. Sprinkle the
seeds into the groove and cover with
about 1cm (⅜in) of soil. Water well and
watch the sprouts begin to grow – you
can carefully uproot them if you need
to give them more space; they like at

least 10cm (4in) in each direction if possible. Sow a fresh batch every month or so for a continuous harvest throughout the summer.

PLANT IT WITH: Dill needs a lot of space, so keep it by itself or with a similarly thin herb that won't branch into it, such as chives.

WORKS PARTICULARLY WELL WITH: Cucumber, lime, lemon, gherkins, mackerel, red peppers, spring onions, trout.

SUBSTITUTE IT WITH: Borage, chervil, parsley.

CAN BE EATEN: Raw or cooked in sauces.

CHERVIL

———

{Anthriscus cerefolium}

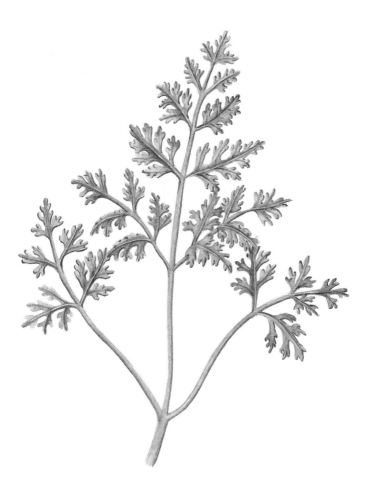

CHERVIL

TASTES: Faintly like liquorice
and similar to parsley.

WHEN TO PLANT: July or August.

WHEN TO PICK: Late autumn to
December. Cut off the leaves, but
leave at least 3cm (1⅛in) of the stem
to allow it to sprout again.

HOW TO PLANT: Chervil will happily
grow in small spaces, in tiny pots or
slotted in among other herbs. Sow the
seeds sparingly, about 5cm (2in) apart,
and cover with a thin layer of compost,
remembering to water well. Thin out

to about 30cm (11¾in) apart. Chervil prefers shade and doesn't like too much heat, so planting it under existing taller plants is a good idea – just make sure that the soil is always a little bit wet.

PLANT IT WITH: Sage, basil, oregano or anything with thick leaves that will help to protect it from the sun.

WORKS PARTICULARLY WELL WITH: Asparagus, duck, fennel, green beans, lamb, potatoes, salmon, trout.

SUBSTITUTE IT WITH: Parsley, oregano, basil.

CAN BE EATEN: Raw or cooked in sauces.

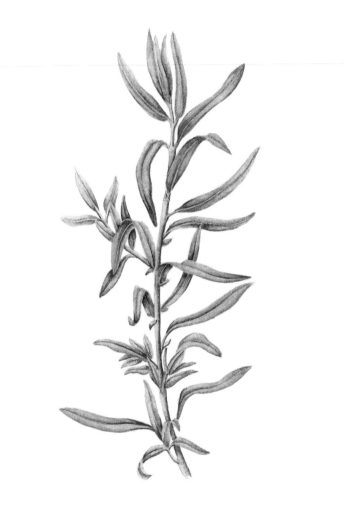

TARRAGON

{Artemisia dracunculus}

TARRAGON

TASTES: Fragrant, like aniseed.

WHEN TO PLANT: Spring to late summer.

WHEN TO PICK: Late spring until late autumn. Snip off the stalks and pinch the leaves.

HOW TO PLANT: Tarragon is one of the easiest herbs to look after – it is hardy and doesn't need much care. It likes a bit of shade, so choose a spot that gets some light but also some respite from the sun. Plant the seeds in shallow dips in the soil, cover with a light dusting of earth and water frequently, making sure the seeds doesn't dry out.

Thin the plants out so that there is 10cm (4in) between each one. Either let it die off in the winter, or bring it indoors where it will live happily on a sunny windowsill.

PLANT IT WITH: Chervil, coriander and chive.

WORKS PARTICULARLY WELL WITH: Chicken, lemon, green peppers, mushrooms, potatoes.

SUBSTITUTE IT WITH: Oregano, lemon balm, chervil.

CAN BE EATEN: Raw, roasted or in sauces.

BORAGE

{Borage officinalis}

BORAGE

—

TASTES: Fresh and cucumber-like.

WHEN TO PLANT: From April to August.

WHEN TO PICK: All the way up until November. You'll mainly want the edible blue flowers, but the leaves go in salads.

HOW TO PLANT: Plant the seeds several centimetres apart, directly into the containers, in a spot that gets a little bit of shade. Cover with a thin layer of soil and water well. Borage doesn't like dry conditions, so make sure the soil is kept moist, but not over-watered. Thin out to about 60cm (24in) apart and keep it as contained as possible – borage

will take over your garden if you let it. The best thing, though, is that as a result it is almost impossible to kill.

PLANT IT WITH: Borage isn't very sociable. Keep it in a medium-sized container so that it has space to grow without taking over everything else.

WORKS PARTICULARLY WELL WITH: Cantaloupe melon, dill, lemon, salmon, spring onions, strawberries, white fish.

SUBSTITUTE IT WITH: Parsley, basil, lemon thyme.

CAN BE EATEN: Raw – it doesn't hold its flavour in cooking.

MUSTARD

———

{Brassicaceae}

MUSTARD

———

TASTES: Hot and peppery.

WHEN TO PLANT: Spring.

WHEN TO PICK: All year round
– it should survive most frosts.

HOW TO PLANT: Create a 0.5cm-
(¼in-) deep groove in the soil with
your finger. Drop the seeds into the
soil, about 2.5cm (1in) apart, and dust
with only the lightest covering of earth.
Water regularly – mustard likes cool
weather and needs to be kept moist,
so a shady spot is ideal. Thin out to
about 15cm (6in) apart once the seeds
have sprouted. Chop off the flowers
of younger plants for use in salads or

stews, and snip the leaves off older plants for salads in place of rocket. During really cold spells it may need to be brought indoors, but some varieties, such as black mustard, thrive on a snap of freezing weather.

PLANT IT WITH: Tall herbs that will offer it shade, such as coriander and oregano.

WORKS PARTICULARLY WELL WITH: Bacon, beef, chicken, garlic, goose, ham, potatoes, radishes.

SUBSTITUTE IT WITH: Nasturtium, winter savory, thyme.

CAN BE EATEN: Raw or stewed in sauces.

CORIANDER

cilantro

———

{Coriandrum sativum}

CORIANDER

———

TASTES: Fresh and citrus-like.

WHEN TO PLANT:
Late spring to the end of August.

WHEN TO PICK: From June through the winter you can tear the leaves off in as big a clump as you would like.

HOW TO PLANT: Make a shallow line-shaped groove in the soil and sprinkle the seeds into it, aiming for a bit of space between each one. Cover with a thin layer of soil and water well. Thin out to 20cm (8in) apart once the seedlings are established. Coriander likes sun but gets burnt and brown in too much heat, so a spot with a bit of shade is ideal. It doesn't grow back particularly strongly after picking the leaves, so plant a new row of seeds every month or so to provide a continuous supply.

PLANT IT WITH: It needs a good amount of water, so pair it with mint, oregano or chives.

WORKS PARTICULARLY WELL WITH: Carrots, chicken, green salad, peanuts, prawns, watermelon, white cabbage.

SUBSTITUTE IT WITH: Mint, basil, lemon balm.

CAN BE EATEN: Raw or cooked in sauces. The seeds can be sprinkled over salads too, or ground to make rubs for meat.

LOVAGE

—

{Levisticum officinale}

LOVAGE

TASTES: Salty and fresh, like celery.

WHEN TO PLANT:
March through to early summer.

WHEN TO PICK: From May until midwinter.

HOW TO PLANT: Create a 2cm-(¾in-) deep groove in the soil with your finger. Sow the lovage seeds about 3cm (1⅛in) apart, cover with a thin layer of soil and water lightly. Thin them out as they grow so that there is about 10cm (4in) between each plant, and water fairly sparingly, keeping the soil damp but not soaked. Lovage can grow really tall unless you prune it regularly – snip the leaves off when you need them and cut it right back in June to encourage further growth. The leaves taste best when they're young, so don't be afraid to hack at larger plants.

PLANT IT WITH: Parsley, basil and oregano.

WORKS PARTICULARLY WELL WITH: Celery, cherries, duck, lettuce, lemon, pasta, red peppers.

SUBSTITUTE IT WITH: Parsley, borage, oregano.

CAN BE EATEN: Raw or cooked in soups and sauces.

LEMON BALM

——

{Melissa officinalis}

LEMON BALM

TASTES: Cool and lemony.

WHEN TO PLANT: Early to late spring,
starting it off indoors first.

WHEN TO PICK: Handfuls of leaves
can be picked off until the very
end of autumn.

HOW TO PLANT: Sow the seeds in small
pots, cover with just a tiny amount of
soil, water well and leave on a sunny
windowsill for a few weeks. Once they
have sprouted and the weather has got a
bit warmer, choose the strongest plants,
uproot them carefully and replant in

pots outside with 10–15cm (4–6in) between each one. Place in a sunny and sheltered spot. Water well throughout the summer and pick the leaves as often as you need – they grow back quickly. Leave out all winter, as it should happily spring back into life the following year.

PLANT IT WITH: Its fresh fragrance will offset more pungent herbs such as chives, but it will get on well with anything that likes sunshine.

WORKS PARTICULARLY WELL WITH: Chicken, courgettes, cucumber, Parmesan, peas, trout.

SUBSTITUTE IT WITH: Lemon thyme, basil, parsley.

CAN BE EATEN: Raw or very lightly cooked and added to pans just before serving.

MINT

———

{Menthe}

MINT

TASTES: Cool and minty.

WHEN TO PLANT: Spring to late summer.

WHEN TO PICK: Late spring to late autumn, and through the winter if it is brought indoors.

HOW TO PLANT: Mint has large roots that can fill a big container, so it's best to plant it by itself. Plant the seeds 5cm (2in) deep and at least 5cm (2in) apart in a very large container. Discard those that are the least promising once they start sprouting. You need to water mint occasionally as it begins to grow, but after that you can leave it to its own devices, giving it more water only during extended droughts. Pick leaves from the top of the plant for eating, and once the mint is about 25–30cm (10–11¾in) tall, start pinching out the top leaves to stop the mint growing up any further. Bring it indoors in the winter and it should keep going as long as you let it.

PLANT IT WITH: Best on its own or with deep-rooted herbs like basil and rosemary.

WORKS PARTICULARLY WELL WITH: Broad beans, cucumber, lamb, lime, mangoes, peas, peaches, prawns.

SUBSTITUTE IT WITH: Lemon balm, parsley, lovage.

CAN BE EATEN: Raw, cooked in sauces or stewed in tea.

BASIL

———

{Ocimum basilicum}

BASIL

———

TASTES: Peppery and sweet.

WHEN TO PLANT: Late spring,
starting off inside.

WHEN TO PICK: Until late September,
removing the leaves from
growing stalks.

HOW TO PLANT: Plant the seeds sparingly
in small pots and cover with a very fine
layer of soil; water well. Leave on a
sunny windowsill. After about 5 weeks,
move them outside, thinning the plants
out until they are about 20cm (8in)
apart. Basil needs sunshine and small
amounts of water often, and will perk

up quickly if it dries out a little. Pinch out the top leaves to stop it from growing too tall.

PLANT IT WITH: Mint, rosemary and thyme for a very fragrant box.

WORKS PARTICULARLY WELL WITH: Chicken, pasta, Parmesan, salmon, peaches, tomatoes.

SUBSTITUTE IT WITH: Mint, lemon balm, oregano.

CAN BE EATEN: Raw or steamed, although it can turn bitter if it is cooked for too long.

MARJORAM

———

{Origanum majorana}

MARJORAM

TASTES: Sweet and pungent, similar to oregano but slightly stronger.

WHEN TO PLANT: Spring.

WHEN TO PICK: Chop off the leaves before the plant flowers in late summer.

HOW TO PLANT: Create a 2cm- (¾in-) deep groove in the soil with your finger. Plant the seeds in a row about 5cm apart. Cover with a very thin layer of earth and water well. You'll need to keep the soil moist for the first couple of weeks until the seed sprouts, then you can start to water less. Marjoram likes sunny climates, so keep it somewhere warm and sheltered, and just prune off the leaves when you need it. It doesn't usually survive cold, wet winters, so either let it die off or bring its container indoors and leave it on a sunny ledge until the following spring.

PLANT IT WITH: Basil and oregano have the same desire for sunshine and don't like too much water.

WORKS PARTICULARLY WELL WITH: Butternut squash, fennel, lamb, onion, pasta, potatoes, spinach.

SUBSTITUTE IT WITH: Oregano, basil, sage.

CAN BE EATEN: Raw or cooked gently in sauces.

OREGANO

———

{Origanum vulgare}

OREGANO

TASTES: Like a milder version of basil.

WHEN TO PLANT: Spring.

WHEN TO PICK: Cut off the leaves
all summer long – this will
encourage more growth.

HOW TO PLANT: Create a 3cm- (1⅛in-)
deep groove in the soil with your finger.
Plant the seeds in the groove, cover
with soil and a light sprinkling of water
and place the pot in an area that gets
a lot of sunlight. As the shoots begin
to sprout, thin them out so that they
are about 10cm (4in) apart, discarding
the weediest stalks. Water frequently
and pinch out the top leaves once they

reach about 20–25cm (8–10in). Chop off any flower buds before they bloom, as they will weaken the flavour of the leaves. Prune oregano right back to just a couple of tiers of leaves and cover with mulch in the winter – it can last anywhere from two to four years.

PLANT IT WITH: Chervil, coriander and lavender.

WORKS PARTICULARLY WELL WITH: Ham, lamb, mozzarella, mushrooms, sausage meat, sea bass, tomatoes.

SUBSTITUTE IT WITH: Basil, marjoram, chervil.

CAN BE EATEN: Raw or cooked in sauces.

PARSLEY

——

{Petroselinim crispum}

PARSLEY

———

TASTES: Like peppery grass.

WHEN TO PLANT: Spring.

WHEN TO PICK: All summer and into autumn, chopping off the stalks and leaves whenever you need them.

HOW TO PLANT: Because parsley seeds are tough, the trick is to soak them in boiling water for a day before you plant them, to break down their exterior. Drain the water away and sprinkle the seeds lightly over the top of your soil, mixing them gently into the surface with your finger. Place the pot in a relatively sunny spot. Water them well, keeping them moist as they sprout and thinning

them out if you have too many. It needs
a gap of at least 5cm (2in) either side
of each to flourish properly. Parsley
usually lasts for two years if you bring
the container indoors over the winter –
you should get pretty flowers in its
second season.

PLANT IT WITH: Oregano, basil,
lemon balm.

WORKS PARTICULARLY WELL WITH:
Cod, lemon, ham, haddock,
mint, Parmesan, potatoes.

SUBSTITUTE IT WITH:
Lemon balm, oregano, basil.

CAN BE EATEN: Raw or cooked in sauces.

PURSLANE

———

{Portulaca oleracea}

PURSLANE

TASTES: Slightly sour and slightly salty.

WHEN TO PLANT: April through to August.

WHEN TO PICK: Snip off the leaves throughout the summer until early autumn.

HOW TO PLANT: Create a series of 1cm- (⅜in-) deep holes in the soil with your finger. Sow the seeds into the holes, cover with a thin layer of soil and water well. Place the container in a sunny spot. Keep watering regularly and you should be able to pick the leaves in less than two months. Purslane will survive in fairly dry conditions, so it is ideal if you want a low-maintenance herb. Just thin out the shoots so that there is about 10cm (4in) between each one, using the weedier plants as micro-greens in a salad. Plant a new crop every month to keep you going throughout the summer.

PLANT IT WITH: Lavender, rosemary, sorrel.

WORKS PARTICULARLY WELL WITH: Apples, mangetout, mangoes, peas, pears, salmon.

SUBSTITUTE IT WITH: Borage, lemon balm, mint.

CAN BE EATEN: Raw or cooked lightly in sauces.

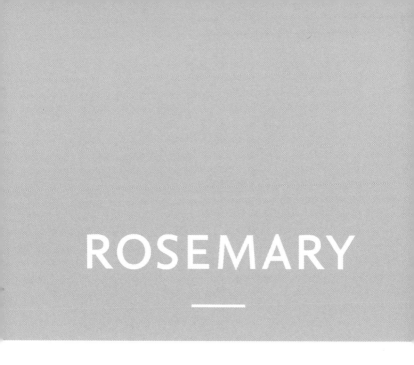

ROSEMARY

———

{Rosmarinus officinalis}

ROSEMARY

TASTES: Pungently aromatic, and similar to pine needles.

WHEN TO PLANT: Late spring.

WHEN TO PICK: Year round, cutting off 8–10cm (3⅓–4in) sprigs.

HOW TO PLANT: Although you can grow rosemary from seed, its success rate is so low that it's best to pot from an existing plant. Dig a hole in a container that is slightly larger and deeper than the pot it came in. Add about 1cm (⅜in) of sand to the hole and put the plant on top, filling it in with the soil you dug out. It won't need much care – just water if it completely dries out and trim the side stems to keep it the size you want. The rosemary will grow as large as you'll let it and should last for up to 20 years with only minimal pruning.

PLANT IT WITH: Other deep-rooted perennial herbs such as thyme, basil and mint.

WORKS PARTICULARLY WELL WITH: Apples, beef, butternut squash, cherries, grapefruit, lamb, lemon, oranges.

SUBSTITUTE IT WITH: Sage, thyme, savory.

CAN BE EATEN: Raw or cooked, and roasts well.

SORREL

——

{Rumex acetosa}

SORREL

—

TASTES: Lemony.

WHEN TO PLANT: March to May.

WHEN TO PICK: Snip off the young leaves from spring through to November.

HOW TO PLANT: Create 0.5cm- (¼in-) deep ridges in the soil using your finger. Sow the seeds, cover them with a sprinkling of soil and water well. Leave the container in a sunny but sheltered spot. Once the seeds have started sprouting, thin them out so that there is 7–8cm (2¾–3⅛in) between each. A few weeks later, once they start to get really thick, thin them out again so that there is a 30cm (11¾in) gap between each one. Regularly prune back the older, larger leaves – they're less tasty anyway and this will encourage new growth. Keep the ground fairly well watered in sunny periods and you should have a very healthy, happy herb on your hands.

PLANT IT WITH: Lavender, rosemary and purslane.

WORKS PARTICULARLY WELL WITH: Chicken, courgettes, cucumber, oranges, strawberries, sea bass, sole.

SUBSTITUTE IT WITH: Lemon thyme, lemon balm, mint.

CAN BE EATEN: Raw, cooked or roasted.

SAGE

{Salvia officinalis}

SAGE

———

TASTES: Earthy and strong.

WHEN TO PLANT: Early spring
or throughout the summer.

WHEN TO PICK: From late
spring until late autumn.

HOW TO PLANT: Create 1cm-
(⅜in-) deep grooves in the soil with
your finger. Sprinkle the seeds into the
grooves, cover with soil and water well.
They should start to shoot up after two
weeks and have leaves ready to pick
after about a month. Thin to 40–55cm
(15¾–21⅝in) apart. When they are
young they need a lot of water, but
once they get bigger you can leave

them in the sunshine and they'll thrive
– just make sure you water them
when they get dry. Sage tends to grow
outwards and take over containers,
so chop off leaves regularly to keep it
the size you want – it's very hardy
and will grow back no matter how
ruthlessly you prune it.

PLANT IT WITH:
Rosemary, basil and oregano.

WORKS PARTICULARLY WELL WITH:
Apples, capers, eggs, green beans,
lamb, pork, tomatoes.

SUBSTITUTE IT WITH:
Marjoram, basil, nasturtium.

CAN BE EATEN: Raw, but it's better
when lightly cooked in sauces.

SUMMER SAVORY

{Satureja hortensis}

SUMMER SAVORY

TASTES: Woody and aromatic, similar to rosemary.

WHEN TO PLANT: March until August.

WHEN TO PICK: You can pick the leaves as soon as they sprout, until about October.

HOW TO PLANT: Create 1cm (⅜in) deep grooves in the soil and scatter the seeds into them, covering with a light dusting of earth. Position the container in a sunny spot and water fairly well, continuing to do so to prevent it from drying out. It can grow outwards and

take over, so thin the shoots out so
that there is a 12cm (5in) space
between each one. Regularly prune
the leaves, pinching them back to
encourage new growth. Savory pretty
hard to kill, so as long as it gets light
and water it should be fine.

PLANT IT WITH: Lavender,
sorrel and oregano.

WORKS PARTICULARLY WELL WITH:
Beef, grapefruit, onions, oranges,
pork, rice, sweet potatoes.

SUBSTITUTE IT WITH:
Rosemary, winter savory, thyme.

CAN BE EATEN: Raw, roasted,
dried or cooked in sauces.

WINTER SAVORY

{Satureja montana}

WINTER SAVORY

TASTES: Peppery. It is a stronger version of summer savory.

WHEN TO PLANT: September.

WHEN TO PICK: All through the winter.

HOW TO PLANT: As its name suggests, winter savory can survive very cold climates, and will even be ok under a snowfall. Create 1cm- (⅜in-) deep grooves in the soil using your finger. Shake the seeds into the grooves, covering with a light sprinkling of soil. Water it straight away and then let the autumnal weather keep the soil moist

– only top it up with water if there is an unseasonable dry spell. Thin out the plants so that there are at least 10cm (4in) gaps between each one and hack at the leaves as much as you like; it will keep growing back as long as you let it. It is perennial, meaning it should keep going, as long as you give it some shade in the summer.

PLANT IT WITH: Violet, parsley and sage.

WORKS PARTICULARLY WELL WITH: Apple, carrots, garlic, pears, sausage meat, white beans.

SUBSTITUTE IT WITH:
Summer savory, rosemary, thyme.

CAN BE EATEN: Raw, roasted or cooked in sauces.

LEMON
THYME

—

{Thymus citriodorus}

LEMON THYME

TASTES: Woody and lemony.

WHEN TO PLANT: Spring.

WHEN TO PICK:
Early summer until late autumn.

HOW TO PLANT: Lemon thyme will spread quite wide, so plant the seeds about 10cm (4in) apart in a shallow well of soil, covering with just a little sprinkling of extra soil, and water well. It likes a lot of sun, water and shelter, and is pretty hardy if it is placed somewhere it can get all three of these. It will flower in high summer, and the flowers can be eaten too; just chop them off and sprinkle them into salads or over meats. The more you pick lemon thyme sprigs, the more you will encourage it to grow, so don't be afraid of hacking away at the leaves or of discarding any woody stalks.

PLANT IT WITH: Its fragrance and sun-worshipping nature make it an ideal partner for lavender, rosemary and regular thyme.

WORKS PARTICULARLY WELL WITH: Apples, chicken, courgettes, elderflower, ginger, pears, turkey.

SUBSTITUTE IT WITH: Lemon balm, thyme, rosemary.

CAN BE EATEN: Raw, roasted, cooked in sauces or steamed with vegetables.

THYME

———

{Thymus vulgaris}

THYME

———

TASTES: Pungently woody.

WHEN TO PLANT: April and throughout the summer.

WHEN TO PICK: Harvest the leaves from midsummer through to late autumn.

HOW TO PLANT: Thyme likes a lot of sun, so it's best to wait until the spring is well underway and the ground has warmed up after the winter. Create 1cm- (⅜in-) deep grooves in the soil with your finger. Plant the seeds in the grooves and cover them with a light sprinkling of soil. Thyme doesn't need too much water, so just make sure it doesn't completely dry out and it should thrive. Pinch back the leaves to stop it from taking over the container – fully-grown plants need at least a 10cm (4in) gap between each one. You can leave them out in the winter; just prune them back to encourage growth.

PLANT IT WITH: Lemon thyme, lavender and rosemary.

WORKS PARTICULARLY WELL WITH: Apples, artichokes, Cheddar cheese, lamb, lemon, ginger, rhubarb, sausage, strawberries.

SUBSTITUTE IT WITH: Savory, rosemary, nasturtium.

CAN BE EATEN: Raw, cooked or roasted.

the
FLOWERS

MARIGOLD

———

{Calendula officinalis}

MARIGOLD

TASTES: Peppery and radish-like.

WHEN TO PLANT: Early spring,
any time after the last frost.

WHEN TO PICK: Throughout the summer.
Lopping off the flower heads will make
the plant grow more replacements.

HOW TO PLANT: Sow the seeds directly
into the containers, covering them with
a thin layer of soil – if you sow new
seeds every three weeks or so, you'll
have a continuous supply. Cover with a
thin layer of soil; water well. Marigolds
like sunshine, water and any fertilising
compost or plant feed you care to give
them. Their roots are not deep, so one

plant to a medium-sized container, or several in a larger one, about 20–40cm (8–15¾in) apart, will be fine. Just make sure it doesn't dry out.

PLANT IT WITH: Lavender, rosemary and mint all like similar conditions and will look really pretty together.

WORKS PARTICULARLY WELL WITH: Beef, blue cheese, butter, celery, chilli, courgettes, olive oil, rice, salt.

SUBSTITUTE IT WITH: Nasturtium, thyme, sage.

CAN BE EATEN: Raw, but works better cooked – oil and oily dishes bring out its full flavour.

HIBISCUS

——

{Hisbiscus rosa-sinensis}

HIBISCUS

TASTES: Fresh and ever so slightly floral.

WHEN TO PLANT: Spring.

WHEN TO PICK: Pick off the edible flower heads throughout summer and autumn; this will encourage more to bloom.

HOW TO PLANT: It's best to buy a baby hibiscus plant rather than trying to grow it from seed. Plant the shrub in a container at least 20cm (8in) in diameter and 20cm (8in) deep, patting soil in around the root ball and leaving the top 2cm (¾in) of it exposed. Hibiscus likes a lot of sun, so grow it in a container that you can easily move around into the light. Don't over-water;

check the soil with your finger for dryness before you add more. Prune any yellow or brown leaves, and move it back indoors for winter – it's very hardy and should survive happily by a sunny window.

PLANT IT WITH: Because its roots grow so wide, it should be kept in its own container.

WORKS PARTICULARLY WELL WITH: Chilli, carrots, cinnamon, ginger, pork, mangoes, milk, oranges, tomatoes.

SUBSTITUTE IT WITH: Mint, violet, honeysuckle.

CAN BE EATEN: Raw, dried or boiled in teas and sauces.

JASMINE

———

{Jasminum}

JASMINE

TASTES: Delicate and tea-like.

WHEN TO PLANT: Spring, after the last frost.

WHEN TO PICK: Chop off the edible flowers throughout the summer.

HOW TO PLANT: Buy a jasmine vine from a garden centre and replant in a larger pot for a few weeks. Then choose a deep container, at least 40cm (15¾in) tall, with a hole in the bottom for drainage. Put some pebbles into the bottom of the container and soak the root ball well with water before dropping it into the pot so that the root is 3cm (1⅛in) from the top. Surround it with soil. Jasmine loves sunshine, so plant it in a bright spot that is sheltered from the wind, preferably in front of a wall or trellis for it to creep up. Keep it well watered and moist.

PLANT IT WITH: Keep jasmine alone in its container. However, the creeping plant will provide good shade for herbs such as borage or chervil nearby.

WORKS PARTICULARLY WELL WITH: Chard, goat's cheese, lemon, salmon, tomatoes.

SUBSTITUTE IT WITH:
Lilac, nasturtium, thyme.

CAN BE EATEN: Raw or boiled in teas.

LAVENDER

—

{Lavendula}

LAVENDER

TASTES: As it smells – floral and sweet.

WHEN TO PLANT: Late winter,
starting it off indoors first.

WHEN TO PICK: The edible flower
heads can be picked from late spring
throughout the summer. More will
grow in their place.

HOW TO PLANT: Cuttings are the
easiest way to grow lavender – you
want a 10cm (4in) side stalk that isn't
flowering. Strip off the bottom leaves
and dip the cut end into a root-growth
stimulator. Plant it at a 5cm (2in) depth
in a small pot of gritty compost and
keep it inside on a sunny windowsill.
Keep it well watered. Replant in

a bigger pot and move it outside after a month or so, once it has really started to grow. Leave it somewhere sunny and water it every day throughout the summer, lopping off any dead heads or leaves. It is fairly hardy and will grow as long as you let it – remove the older stems as they get woody and let the new stems keep replenishing themselves.

PLANT IT WITH: Sun-loving, thirsty plants such as oregano, purslane and savory.

WORKS PARTICULARLY WELL WITH: Apricots, beef, lemon, pork, peaches, raspberries.

SUBSTITUTE IT WITH: Violet, rosemary, savory.

CAN BE EATEN: Raw, roasted or boiled in sauces and teas.

HONEYSUCKLE

—

{Lonicera}

HONEYSUCKLE

TASTES: Sweet, like honey.

WHEN TO PLANT: Spring.

WHEN TO PICK: Pick off the edible flower heads from high summer all the way through to mid-autumn.

HOW TO PLANT: Growing from seed is tricky, so it's much easier to start from cuttings. These will grow up trellises and walls very happily in sunlight. If your variety is a climber, plant the cutting in a deep container next to a wall in full sunlight. If it's a bush variety, plant it anywhere that gets a lot of warmth. Add a touch of root-growth stimulator to the base of the cutting and keep its soil well watered. Prune the flowers to keep it the shape and size you want, as honeysuckle tends to ramble and take over... which is really part of its charm.

PLANT IT WITH: Honeysuckle needs space to grow but it will attract bees, so plant lavender nearby to really draw them to your edible garden.

WORKS PARTICULARLY WELL WITH: Blackberries, blackcurrants, honey, ginger, maple syrup, mint.

SUBSTITUTE IT WITH: Mint, hibiscus, rose.

CAN BE EATEN: Raw or boiled in sauces and teas.

GERANIUM

{Pelargonium}

GERANIUM

TASTES: Subtly floral.

WHEN TO PLANT:
April, starting the plants off indoors.

WHEN TO PICK: Break off the scented leaves from summer until late autumn.

HOW TO PLANT: Fill a pot with soil and sprinkle over a few seeds of a scented-leaved geranium, leaving about 2.5cm (1in) between them. Cover with a dusting of soil – try to keep it all quite loose. Add a bit of water and some liquid fertiliser and set on a sunny windowsill for a few weeks. Once sprouted, and spring's temperamental weather is out of the way, move them outside – they

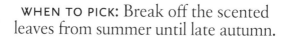

like a lot of sunshine, so put them in the brightest spot. Don't water too often; check the soil with your finger, and if it's still moist, leave them be. Chop off any dead heads or brown leaves, and bring them back indoors at the end of September to the sunniest part of your house.

PLANT IT WITH: It is best kept on its own, but it looks pretty when you include different varieties and colours.

WORKS PARTICULARLY WELL WITH: Lemon, melon, raspberries, sponge cake, strawberries.

SUBSTITUTE IT WITH: Rose, violet, savory.

CAN BE EATEN: Cooked – their leaves give off flavour at high temperatures.

LILAC

{Syringa}

LILAC

TASTES: More peppery than floral, not unlike radish.

WHEN TO PLANT: Spring to early summer.

WHEN TO PICK: The edible flower heads can be picked all through the summer.

HOW TO PLANT: You'll want to start this off from a baby plant bought in a garden centre. You will need a larger pot with a hole in the bottom for drainage. Put some pebbles into the bottom of the container and soak the root ball well with water before planting. Choose a sunny spot and don't overcrowd – it likes a lot of space in its pot. If you never let the soil get soggy and you remove any dead heads, then the lilac should bloom very happily; just give it a drop of plant food every couple of weeks in the spring and summer to keep it strong.

PLANT IT WITH: It prefers its own pot and space, but it is so colourful that you can plant it near lavender and nasturtiums to make a really pretty collection.

WORKS PARTICULARLY WELL WITH: Blackberries, blackcurrants, cream cheese, grouse, lemon, sea bass.

SUBSTITUTE IT WITH: Nasturtium, calendula, thyme.

CAN BE EATEN: Raw, cooked or stewed.

NASTURTIUM

—

{Tropaeolum}

NASTURTIUM

TASTES: Peppery, with a hint of citrus.

WHEN TO PLANT: Early spring, starting it off indoors first.

WHEN TO PICK: All summer long, until late September. The seeds in the dead heads can be used like capers.

HOW TO PLANT: Start them off indoors on a sunny windowsill. Fill a medium-sized container with soil and plant the seeds about 3cm (1⅛in) deep, 8–10 seeds to a pot. Cover with a thin layer of soil and water well. Water them regularly and after about a month choose the two or three sprouts that look the strongest and discard the rest.

Move the pot outside to as sunny a spot as possible and don't add any fertiliser, as they bloom better without it. Cut off any dead heads throughout the summer and the plants probably won't need any pruning.

PLANT IT WITH: Nasturtium tends to ramble, so keep it alone or go for fairly contained herbs such as chives.

WORKS PARTICULARLY WELL WITH:
Artichokes, cabbage, celery, white fish.

SUBSTITUTE IT WITH:
Calendula, thyme, basil.

CAN BE EATEN:
Raw or steamed with vegetables.

VIOLET

{Viola}

VIOLET

TASTES: Floral and slightly soapy.

WHEN TO PLANT: Autumn.

WHEN TO PICK: Late winter through to early summer.

HOW TO PLANT: You can buy violet plants from the garden centre, but if you are starting from seed, then plant them when the weather starts to cool. Do not buy African violets (*Saintpaulia*) as they are inedible. Make 2cm- (¾in-) deep holes in the soil that are at least 5–10cm (2–4in) apart. Sow the seeds and cover with a thin layer of soil. Water immediately, but then leave them over the winter to quietly germinate.

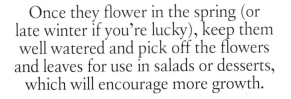

Once they flower in the spring (or late winter if you're lucky), keep them well watered and pick off the flowers and leaves for use in salads or desserts, which will encourage more growth.

PLANT IT WITH: As the herbs begin to die off in the autumn, replace them with violets – you can switch them back the following summer.

WORKS PARTICULARLY WELL WITH: Cream, cinnamon, grapefruit, lemon, plums.

SUBSTITUTE IT WITH:
Rose, lavender, geranium.

CAN BE EATEN: Raw or cooked.

PANSY

———

{Viola tricolor hortensis}

PANSY

TASTES: Vaguely salty and slightly peppery, with an underlying savoury flavour.

WHEN TO PLANT:
Late spring to midsummer.

WHEN TO PICK: Remove the edible flower heads throughout the summer.

HOW TO PLANT: If it's still quite cool outside, start the pansies off indoors, otherwise plant them straight into a container in a really sunny spot. Make a series of 2cm- (¾in-) deep holes in the soil using your finger, put a seed into each and cover with soil. Keep the soil well watered and the seeds should

sprout within about three weeks. The more times you pick off the flowers for salads, the more they'll grow, so don't be afraid to really attack them. Lop off any brown leaves and if you keep them well watered they should do well all season.

PLANT IT WITH: Other sun-loving plants such as rosemary, lavender and thyme.

WORKS PARTICULARLY WELL WITH: Cabbage, carrots, coriander, lime, radishes, trout, tuna.

SUBSTITUTE IT WITH: Nasturtium, calendula, thyme.

CAN BE EATEN: Raw in salads.

INDEX

For nanna and grandma, who both loved
flowers, though might have been surprised
that I'd want to eat them.

PUBLISHING DIRECTOR Sarah Lavelle
CREATIVE DIRECTOR Helen Lewis
EDITOR Harriet Butt
DESIGNER Gemma Hayden
ILLUSTRATOR Louise O'Reilly
PRODUCTION Vincent Smith, Emily Noto

First published in 2017 by
Quadrille Publishing Limited
Pentagon House
52 Southwark Street
London SE1 1UN
www.quadrille.co.uk
www.quadrille.com

Text © 2014 Pip McCormac
Illustration © 2016 Louise O'Reilly
Design and layout © 2016
Quadrille Publishing Limited

Cataloguing in Publication Data:
a catalogue record for this book is
available from the British Library.

ISBN 978 1 84949 939 2

Printed in China